Raising Successful Children

A Guide for Christian Parents

Pastors (Dr.) Zacch I. Olorunnipa

&

(Mrs.) Florence O. Olorunnipa

Raising Successful Children

Copyright © 2019 by Pastors (Dr.) Zacch I. Olorunnipa & (Mrs.) Florence O. Olorunnipa

All rights reserved. No part of this book may be reproduced or transmitted in any form or by any means without written permission of the author.

Scriptures marked KJV are taken from the KING JAMES VERSION (KJV): KING JAMES VERSION, public domain.

Scriptures marked NAS are taken from the NEW AMERICAN STANDARD (NAS): Scripture taken from the NEW AMERICAN STANDARD BIBLE®, copyright© 1960, 1962, 1963, 1968, 1971, 1972, 1973, 1975, 1977, 1995 by The Lockman Foundation. Used by permission. Scriptures marked NIV are taken from the NEW INTERNATIONAL VERSION (NIV): Scripture taken from THE HOLY BIBLE, NEW INTERNATIONAL VERSION ®. Copyright© 1973, 1978, 1984, 2011 by Biblica, Inc.™. Used by permission of Zondervan

Published by:
Eleviv Publishing Group
Houston, TX 77082

ISBN: 978-1-7331416-4-2

10 9 8 7 6 5 4 3 2 1

This book is dedicated to the memory of our parents:

Chief and Mrs. Benjamin Olorunnipa
and
Chief and Mrs. Jethro Osanaiye

and to our children:

Oluwafunmilayo E. Olorunnipa
(Grad. of University of Florida, University of California-Berkeley School of Law, Harvard University-Kennedy School of Government)

Olushola B. Olorunnipa
(Grad. of Harvard University; Stanford University School of Medicine)

Toluse O. Olorunnipa
(Grad. of Stanford University; Stanford University Graduate School)

Zacch Opeyemi Olorunnipa
(Grad. of Princeton University)

Table of Contents

Acknowledgments
Preamble
God's Plan for Children's Education 1
Parents' Role in Children's Education 7
Tools for Success in Children's Education 13
Praying for and Prophesying Over Your Children 23
About the Authors

Acknowledgments

There are countless reasons why we must thank God for making it possible for us to write this book. The book would not have materialized if God had not created us, saved us, spared our lives, and allowed us to grow up, become educated, get married, have children, come to America, and raise and educate our children. For these possibilities and so many others, we say *"Blessing, and glory, and wisdom, and thanksgiving, and honour, and power, and might, be unto our God for ever and ever. Amen" (Rev. 7:12).*

We are immensely grateful to the "Barnabases" in our lives who not only encouraged us to write the book, but who reminded us persistently to "just do it." Their tenacity and love for our family has contributed significantly to the creation of this book, and we are thankful to all of you. Foremost among those who encouraged the writing of this book is Deaconess Joyce Peterside, who for years has been a faithful ministry partner and a great admirer of our children, and who has made several prophetic declarations on them. We greatly appreciate your prayers and support for our family.

Great commendation also goes to various ministries of which our family has been a part over the years. Ministries such as the Presbyterian Church in Illinois, Unity Baptist Church, Redeemed Christian Church, International Chapel, RCCG, and Go Ye Chapel have provided solid environments for the development and growth of our children's faith in the Lord Jesus Christ. To the leaders and members of these churches, we say, "thank you."

Our wonderful children (Funmi, Shola, Toluse, and Yemi) deserve special commendation and thanks. Your obedience, ingenuity, hard work, endurance, understanding, cooperation, and many other attributes, have made the work of raising and training you quite easy. We are grateful to

God for bringing you into this world through us. We appreciate and thank you, and we are proud of you.

    Thanks again to my publisher, Vivian Elebiyo, who acted promptly to do an excellent job to ensure the timely publishing of this book.

PREAMBLE

"So then it is not of him that willeth, nor of him that runneth, but of God that sheweth mercy" (Romans 9:16).

It is God's mercy that has made the writing of this book possible. When we think of the innumerable things that God, by His mercy, has done for our family, we are most humbly grateful and indebted to Him. Foremost among the things that God's mercy has made possible in our lives are our salvation, the blessing of a wonderful family, and the education of our children. To God be all the glory.

The motivation to write this book came from two sources: first, some Christian brothers, sisters, and friends of ours who felt that God has helped our family succeed in educating our four children. These wonderful friends have encouraged us to document the strategies, tips, and experiences that have proven helpful in molding the academic character of our children and contributed to their successes. We have decided to make this effort to honor the wishes of our beloved Christian brothers, sisters, and friends.

Our secondary motivation came from our own personal awe as to how God has lifted our heads from abject poverty and blessed us with the opportunity to come to the United States of America. Without God's grace, we could never have received this opportunity. It is no exaggeration to say that poverty defined our backgrounds. We both had poor, illiterate parents who lived in poor villages in Africa, lacking the most basic of amenities, such as hospitals, clinics, secondary schools, pipe-borne water, and electricity.

As loving as our parents were, they were too poor to send their children to well-equipped schools. We both went to non-boarding secondary schools, and our living conditions were very harsh. We met in 1973 and were married in 1980. A bit of information about our backgrounds is in order at this point.

Zacch's Educational Background

Until Zacch was six-years-old, he spent most of his time learning and working on his father's farm, along with his many brothers and sisters from his large, polygamous family. A major turning point in Zacch's life occurred when he was "released" to a friend of his parents, who offered to help raise Zacch in his own village, some 20 miles away. The friend needed a child to put in school so that he could benefit from the taxes he was paying to maintain the primary school in his village. That is how Zacch started school—a new experience in a new environment, under a new, loving guardian.

Zacch did very well in primary school, leading his class intermittently during his seven years there. After finishing primary school, Zacch was accepted to a mission secondary school with no boarding facility, located two miles away. He had to walk to school daily. After scraping together, the school fees, his parents had precious little left over to pay for his food, other than a few raw yams he could bring from his village at the beginning of the school term.

Without money to buy many clothes, Zacch had to make do with one pair of short pants and one shirt, and one school uniform. When the clothes were dirty, Zacch would wait for a sunny day to wash them, wearing one outfit while the other was drying in the sun, then washing the other when the first one was dry.

While in secondary school, Zacch's faith in God was strengthened through the Fellowship of Christian Students (FCS), of which he was an active member. Through prayer and hard work, his academic performance improved, and many of his instructors liked him. Over the weekends, he did garden work and house cleaning for some of the foreign instructors to earn money to help with his basic needs.

Zacch was fortunate to be one of the few students to receive a merit-based partial scholarship from the school, which helped pay part of his fees. Unfortunately, the school was unable to continue the scholarship due to lack of funds.

After Zacch completed his secondary education, he went on to complete his Higher School Certificate (HSC) studies. Upon completing his HSC studies, Zacch taught in a secondary school for nine months, during which time he met Florence. Zacch left the secondary school for college on a government scholarship to begin studies for his undergraduate degree.

Florence's Educational Background

Florence embarked upon her education late due to factors beyond her control. At age 11, she enrolled herself in elementary school, where she progressed rapidly, skipping grades several times due to her excellent performance.

Florence gained admission to a secondary school in her village. The school was new and lacked essential educational amenities such as a laboratory and a library. Florence also experienced challenges. She lived in her family compound, which was about a mile and a half from her school, and she also walked to school every day. Her family was very poor, and she suffered hunger many days, occasionally eating one meal per day, on "lucky days." Unable to afford bar soap, she would use leftover powdered laundry detergent to take her bath.

After graduating from secondary school, Florence worked for a time before entering a college of technology to take preparatory courses to secure admission to the university. In 1980, following seven years of courtship, she was married to Zacch, after which she began her university studies. Our first two children were born while Florence was pursuing her undergraduate degree.

Background of Poverty Turned into a Blessing

With respect to our lives in general and education in particular, our case is a laboratory platform for the manifestation of the word of God that says, *"And we know that all things work together for good to them that love God, to them who are the called according to his purpose" (Rom 8:28)*. We owe God an incalculable debt of gratitude for all the ways He transformed our lives, from very poor beginnings to what we consider a happy and successful ending, especially regarding the impact it has had on training our children.

Our humble origins motivated our desire and determination that, God willing, our children would have the best educational training possible. We did not want them to suffer what we experienced in poorly equipped secondary schools. God fulfilled our desire and determination regarding our children's education. This process began when Zacch was blessed with an opportunity to come to the United States.

As mentioned earlier, Zacch had the opportunity to do some domestic work for the foreign teachers at his secondary school. This interaction motivated him to pursue opportunities for Western education. Although Nigerian education in those days was sound, Zacch had the desire and ambition to expand his educational experience by studying abroad.

God took note of Zacch's desire and answered his prayer as Zacch was granted admission to the U.S. to pursue his doctorate, following the completion of his B.S. and M.S. degrees in Nigeria. Later, Zacch's family joined him in the U.S. By the grace of God and with the support of Zacch's family, today he is a U.S. trained Ph.D. holder and retired professor, after 28 years teaching at a U.S. university. Thanks be to God, who has been our support throughout our educational journeys.

Almighty God turned our stories to glory such that our poverty became a platform for promotion, and today we are blessed to be pastors and parents of four wonderful children, all of them Ivy-League-trained graduates in the most advanced country in the world. As part of our gratitude to God, we are compelled to share the techniques of our God-ordained success and survival strategies in raising our children. We believe that this narrative will not only glorify God, but also prove useful to the many people who may desire similar blessings to those we have received. We are grateful to God for the favor we have received from Him, and to so many good people whom God has used to help our family on our journey.

As parents, we all want our children to be healthy and successful for the following reasons:

- Healthy, successful children are a fulfillment of God's promise (Jer. 29:11).
- It can make parents and other people proud, and it can make significant contributions to the society, spiritually, socially, economically, culturally, and educationally.
- These contributions can span local, national, and global boundaries.
- Successful children can become innovators who can help promote economic development.
- They can be a blessing to themselves and to their world.

In recent times, raising successful children in a Godly way has become an uphill task, due to myriad societal vices, many of which have resulted largely from the Biblical warning that, "in the last days perilous times shall come. *2 For men shall be lovers of their own selves, covetous, boasters, proud, blasphemers, disobedient to parents, unthankful, unholy 3 Without natural affection, trucebreakers, false accusers, incontinent, fierce, despisers of those that are good, 4 Traitors, heady, high-minded, lovers of pleasures more than lovers of God; 5 Having a form of godliness, but denying the power thereof: from such turn away"(2 Tim 3:1-5)*. Examples of vices that tend to complicate raising Godly children include peer pressure, pornography, alcoholism, drug addiction, violence, crime, deterioration of family values, negative media influence, disobedience to parents, teaching of evolution and humanism in schools, disrespect for authority, promiscuity, and so on.

Parents from developing or "third-world" countries who live in advanced nations face unique barriers that pose additional challenges to childrearing, particularly in terms of cultural shocks, language barriers emanating from differences in accents, and weather-related hazards.

The role of sound education in raising successful children cannot be overemphasized. The dictionary defines "education" as "the act or process of imparting or acquiring general knowledge, developing the powers of reasoning and judgment, and generally of preparing oneself or others intellectually for mature life." Education has spiritual, social, economic and other benefits to individuals and to the society. It is no wonder that the Bible strongly advocates the need to provide our children with sound education. The Holy Spirit, through King Solomon, declares, *"Train up a child in the way he should go: and when he is old, he will not depart from it"* (Pro 22:6). Apostle Paul, one of the most educated persons in the Bible, advised Timothy, his protégé, along with other believers, to *"Study to shew thyself approved unto God, a workman that needeth not to be ashamed, rightly dividing the word of truth"* (2 Tim.2:15).

Education provides ample opportunities to acquire wisdom, which the Bible declares to be the principal objective, along with understanding (Pro 4:7). Also, the Bible declares that, *"Better is it to get wisdom than gold! and to get understanding rather to be chosen than silver!"* (Pro 16:16). Jesus Christ provides a perfect example after which we can model our children's education, given that He is the embodiment of wisdom. In His divine nature, He is *"the power of God, and the wisdom of God"* (1 Cor. 1:24). When He came into this world as a little boy, His parents, Joseph and Mary, must have given him a good foundation in terms of acquiring wisdom. No wonder the Bible declares, that He *"grew, and waxed strong in spirit, filled with wisdom"* (Luke 2:40).

Jesus Christ facilitated his efforts to educate and train him well. He did this by being obedient, studious, hardworking, humble, diligent, devoted, and curious. He demonstrated these qualities on one occasion when he accompanied His parents to Jerusalem during the annual celebration of the Passover feast (Luke 2: 39-52). When the celebration was over and they were returning to Nazareth, Jesus stood behind in the temple unknown to the parents. When they discovered that Jesus was missing, they rushed back to Jerusalem to look for him. The Bible says, "And it came to pass, that after three days they found him in the temple, sitting in the midst of the doctors, both hearing them, and asking them questions. And all that heard him were astonished at his understanding and answers (Luke 2: 46-47). When His parents told Jesus about how they had sorrowfully searched for Him and wondered why He had treated them so, Jesus responded, "How is it that ye sought me? wist ye not that I must be about my Father's business?" (v. 49). Jesus did not joke with the business of His Father, God. That is why He gave 100percent attention to learning all that He needed to succeed in doing the job ahead of Him.

The strategies suggested in this book for raising and educating children successfully are informed largely by the modality seen in the upbringing of Jesus Christ, along with what could be gleaned from the lives of other Biblical characters, such as David, Joseph, Daniel, and Esther. Also, we have embedded additional gems from our own personal experiences that God gave us by His mercy and that have proven very helpful in raising and educating our children.

The fact is that child raising is a divine responsibility, given by God to every parent. Even in this crooked generation, it is still possible to raise children successfully, by trusting God and following His guidelines. It is our earnest prayer that, because Jesus Christ was successfully raised, you and your children shall be very successful, in the mighty name of Jesus.

End of Chapter Prayer Points
1. Father, please bless me as I read this book.
2. Father, if there is any adversity in my background and foundation, turn it into my advantage in Jesus' name.
3. Father, please teach and instruct me how to raise and educate my children in Jesus mighty name.

God's Plan for Children's Education

For I know the plans I have for you," says the LORD. *"They are plans for good and not for disaster, to give you a future and a hope (Jer. 29:11, NLT)*

God has plans for people of all ages, including children. As indicated in the scripture above, God's plans are generally good; they are not meant to bring unhappiness. Furthermore, they can be dynamic and, working together, are expected to further an expected end. The expected end for a true follower of Jesus Christ is the kingdom of God, while for a non-believer it is hell.

Parents who want their children to be successful must know that God has good plans for children even before they are born. A good illustration of this point is the case of Jeremiah, about whom God said, *"Before I formed thee in the belly, I knew thee; and before thou camest forth out of the womb I sanctified thee, and I ordained thee a prophet unto the nations"* (Jer. 1:5). In other words, God had already ordained that Jeremiah would become a prophet, not to one nation, but to nations. Parents must know that God is the real owner of children, and He has good plans for them (Psalm127:3). Therefore, parents who are interested in the success of their children must ensure that the plans of God for children are adequately woven into their secular training plans.

While God's plans for every human being, including children, are many, they can be classified generally into two broad categories: (a) the spiritual plan, and b) the physical plan. Man is tripartite in nature in that he is comprised of spirit, soul, and body. God's spiritual plan for man relates to the spiritual component, while God's physical plan is concerned with his soul and body. Both spiritual and physical plan must be properly and prayerfully integrated into the planning and upbringing and training of children.

God's Spiritual Plan for Children

"But when Jesus saw it, he was much displeased, and said unto them, "Suffer the little children to come unto me, and forbid them not: for of such is the kingdom of God" (Mark 10: 14).

God is deeply interested in the spiritual welfare of every human being, and He wants every person to inherit the Kingdom of heaven. This explains why Jesus Christ said that the kingdom of heaven should rank as number one amongst all the things sought after by His followers: *"But seek ye first the kingdom of God, and his righteousness; and all these things shall be added unto you" (Matt 6:33).* The primary requirement for entering the kingdom of heaven is to have salvation through belief by faith in Jesus Christ (John 3:16, 14:6). Therefore, it is critically important to give your children a solid spiritual foundation by leading them to accept Jesus Christ as their personal Savior. You must also teach them about the values of loving God, studying His word regularly, obeying His statutes and commandments and serving Him diligently. These are consistent with God's expectations as evident from the following scriptures:

"Now these are the commandments, the statutes, and the judgments, which the LORD your God commanded to teach you, that ye might do them in the land whither ye go to possess it: 2 That thou mightest fear the LORD thy God, to keep all his statutes and his commandments, which I command thee, thou, and thy son, and thy son's son, all the days of thy life; and that thy days may be prolonged. 3 Hear therefore, O Israel, and observe to do it; that it may be well with thee, and that ye may increase mightily, as the LORD God of thy fathers hath promised thee, in the land that floweth with milk and honey. 4 Hear, O Israel: The LORD our God is one LORD: 5 And thou shalt love the LORD thy God with all thine heart, and with all thy soul, and with all thy might. 6 And these words, which I command thee this day, shall be in thine heart: 7 And thou shalt teach them diligently unto thy children, and shalt talk of them when thou sittest in thine house, and when thou walkest by the way, and when thou liest down, and when thou risest up" (Deut. 6: 1-7).

Every physical thing has a spiritual origin, including education. Therefore, considerable effort must be made to establish and strengthen the spiritual backgrounds of children whom parents wish to see succeed academically. Children must be taught that God is the giver of the wisdom they will need to succeed in their secular education (James 1: 5-6).

Some of the strategies that parents can use to help young people develop strong faith in God include:

- Presenting God to children as the all-powerful, inevitable "personality," with incomparable virtues of loving, caring, trustworthiness, and in the family.
- Be an example to children as strong believers and followers of Jesus Christ.
- Lead your children to accept Jesus Christ as early as possible.
- Teach children how to trust God and depend on Him for everything, including success.
- Pray regularly with your children (Prayer altar can be helpful).
- Involve your children in as many Christian activities as possible.
- Go over their school work with them daily (or as frequently as possible) with keen interest, and try to point out the role of God as the creator of all things, including school work (Gen 2:15, Ps. 19:1).
- Teach children how to trust and love God and depend on Him for success.
- Help children develop self-confidence that, with God, all things are possible.

By the grace of God, each of our four children began their spiritual journeys with God in the womb, when we (my wife in particular) started praying over them. They were exposed to various Christian activities, such as hearing Christian choruses and songs sung to them, reading the Bible and other Christian literature to them, and playing Christian tapes for them to enjoy.

God's Physical Plan for Children
1. *"And all thy children shall be taught of the LORD; and great shall be the peace of thy children" (Isa.54:13).*
2. *"Train up a child in the way he should go: and when he is old, he will not depart from it" (Pro 2:6).*
3. *"Take fast hold of instruction; let her not go: keep her; for she is thy life" (Pro. 4:13).*
4. *"Wisdom is the principal thing; therefore, get wisdom: and with all thy getting get understanding" (Pro 4:7).*
5. *How much better [is it] to get wisdom than gold! and to get understanding rather to be chosen than silver! (Pro.16:16).*
6. *Take fast hold of instruction; let [her] not go: keep her; for she [is] thy life. (Pro. 4:13).*

Aside from the spiritual realm, God is also interested in the physical dimensions of children, including good health, intellectual development, cultural and socio-economic growth, and general welfare. Children are God's heritage (Ps. 127:3), and they are gifts from God to parents (James 1:17). The physical plans of God for children include the expectation that they grow in stature, wisdom, and other areas. We see the manifestation of this plan in the life of baby Jesus Christ. The Bible says, *"he grew and waxed strong in spirit" and "increased in stature and in wisdom" (Luke 1:80; 2:52).*

Children's education involves helping them acquire appropriate knowledge, wisdom (the application of knowledge), and skills to prepare them for productive and meaningful lives. God sanctions providing children with sound instruction and education as alluded to the scriptures above. God's interest in proper education of children is evident in what the Bible says about the four Hebrew boys: *"As for these four children, God gave them knowledge and skill in all learning and wisdom: and Daniel had understanding in all visions and dreams" (Daniel 1:17).* God is still in the business of giving children knowledge, skill in all learning and wisdom.

Some of the strategies that can be used to put children on solid and sound secular education include:

- As early as possible, commit children's education to God's care through prayer.
- Become involved personally in instructing, teaching, and training your children.
- Where appropriate, supplement secular educational materials with additional relevant materials.
- Help your children set realistic goals in activities such as reading (learning to read, reading a certain number of books per given period, etc.).
- Take children to the library for study time, and expose them to broad-but-relevant educational materials.
- Help children see the relevance of what they are learning to real-life applications.
- Schedule regular meetings with your children's teachers. Appreciate the work of teachers in words and in kind if you can.
- Study each child closely to identify what they are good at, and encourage him/her as necessary in those areas.

Discourage excessive television watching. Use the time to get children more actively engaged in activities related to potential future career. Volunteer to help in your child's school/class in any area in which they can use your input.

End of Chapter Prayer Points

1. Father, let my children give their lives to you and have keen interest in serving You in Jesus' name.
2. Father, please let your spiritual and physical plans for my children materialize in Jesus' name.
3. Father, give my children spirit of obedience as I explain to them and teach them what to do about Your Physical and Spiritual plans for them, in Jesus' name.

Parents' Role in Children's Education

After God, parents are the most important influences in helping their children build a solid educational foundation. Parents are God's primary representatives to their children for the simple reason that they are the ones used by God to bring their children into existence. It follows that parents are God's first choice in terms of who will administer His spiritual and physical plans for children. This explains why God gave parents and their children the following charges:

"And, ye fathers, provoke not your children to wrath: but bring them up in the nurture and admonition of the Lord" (Eph 6:4).

"My son, hear the instruction of thy father, and forsake not the law of thy mother" (Pro 1:8)

God requires parents, not hired labor, to responsibility in ensuring that their children are brought up in a Godly way. Therefore, parents must cooperate with God in providing their children with sound spiritual and formal education. This should be done carefully, by giving children appropriate instruction about knowing God and obeying His laws. God's instructions to Moses and the Israelites in this regard provide useful guidelines to parents who are looking for success in their children's education:

Therefore, shall ye lay up these my words in your heart and in your soul, and bind them for a sign upon your hand, that they may be as frontlets between your eyes. 19 And ye shall teach them your children, speaking of them when thou sittest in thine house, and when thou walkest by the way, when thou liest down, and when thou risest up (Deut 11:18-19).

This scripture suggests first, that parents take God's words seriously to heart and be doer of the word (not hearer only) before they can teach them to their children effectively. Second, parents are to use every available opportunity to teach the words and ways of God to their children.

Third, there must be no ambiguity in terms of instruction given to children and what is expected of them.

The first example in the Bible of someone who had a thorough understanding of God's expectation in educating children is Abraham, the father of faith. God was so confident about Abraham in this regard that He testified boldly about him, saying: *"For I know him, that he will command his children and his household after him, and they shall keep the way of the Lord, to do justice and judgment; that the Lord may bring upon Abraham that which he hath spoken of him"* (Gen. 18:19).

It is obvious from this scripture that God, who is omniscient, had foreknowledge that Abraham would adopt both spiritual and physical plans of God in raising his children. As He did for Abraham, God still expects present-day parents to "command his children and his household after him, and they shall keep the way of the Lord, to do justice and judgment." One writer explained the phrase "to do justice" as "just conduct, fair dealing, correctness, well-founded reasoning" and "judgment" as "coming to right conclusions, making decisions in the light of consequences, discerning between what is right and wrong, what is acceptable and unacceptable to God" (J. Luke Martin). From This. it is clear that God's educational plan for children calls for comprehensive training, encompassing both spiritual and formal (or physical) training to prepare them for productive Lives.

In general, anyone can be used by God to execute His spiritual and physical plans for training children. However, God's first choice in this regard is usually the biological parents of the child, as they are the ones God used to bring the child into the world. If for some reason the parents are unable or fail to perform the role of training a child, God will find a substitute. Anyone responsible for raising or training a child for success is likely to obtain the best result by using an approach that incorporates into the approach the spiritual and physical agenda of God. Such parents must see themselves as agents of God, expected to play many roles in the lives of their children. Among these roles are the following: minister, model, mentor, motivator, manager, moderator, messenger, and mediator. These functions are explained briefly below:

Parent as Minister

Parents are to serve as God's representatives in their home and let their children know that they are God's heritage and expected to have intimate relationships with Him. Lead your children to Christ and teach them the word of God as instructed in Deut. 11:9 and Josh. 1:9. As much as possible, let them realize that God must be honored in all that they do, including their training and/or education. Along with the word of God, parents are also to minister substance to their children in terms of their physical needs, such as shelter, food, clothing, etc.

Parent as role Model

From birth, children watch their parents, and whatever parents say or do impact their children's lives. Therefore, parents' roles include being good role models to their children. The Bible says, *"And you yourself must be an example to them by doing good works of every kind. Let everything you do reflect the integrity and seriousness of your teaching" (Titus 2: 7, NLT)*. Charles F. Kettering said, "Every father should remember that one day his son will follow his example instead of his advice." With respect to education, read to your children, read with them, let them see you study, and go with them to places that will enrich their educational experience.

Parent as Mentor

The Bible says, "He that walketh with wise [men] shall be wise: but a companion of fools shall be destroyed" (Pro 13:20). You can be the primary mentor to your child while other people with proven integrity and success in specific areas, such as education, can also help mentor your child as you see fit. Encourage your child to associate with wise people.

Parent as Motivator

There is no doubt that children often need motivation. This is an important action that must not be missing in the life of a child destined for success. Parents can motivate their children to engage in things that can enhance their success, such as participation in speaking contest, spelling bee, essay competition, and so on. As the Bible says, parents must ensure that their children are, "not slothful in business; but fervent in spirit" (Rom. 12:11a).

Parent as Manager

The dictionary defines a "manager" as "a person who has control or direction of an institution, business, etc., or of a part, division, or phase of it." Parents are responsible for managing their children's education. This calls for ensuring that the training children receive reflects elements of God's spiritual and physical plans. Also, parents should find out what resources are needed by their children in their educational pursuits. Efforts must then be made to ensure that the resources are available. Help your children manage their time, schedules, energy, and associations. As managers, parents must also administer appropriate discipline to their children with love (Pro 13:24; 22:15; 23:14; 29:15).

Parents as Moderator

Moderators are those who keep things within reasonable or proper limits. One way for parents to ensure children's educational success is to moderate their children's activities. Parents must guide against under-performance in all educational activities while helping their children avoid actions that can put their success in jeopardy. Parents must also help moderate their children's attitudes, character, and communication, to enhance their educational success.

Parent as Mediator

To "mediate" means "to act between parties to facilitate an agreement, compromise, reconciliation, etc." Families with multiple children often face issues such as disputes, sibling rivalry, and conflict, which, if not dealt with immediately, can be disruptive to children's educational progress. Parents can play the role of mediator in such cases to resolve issues and arrive at peaceful reconciliation.

End of Chapter Prayer Points

1. Father, thank You for giving me the grace to be a parent in Jesus name.
2. Father, please don't let me fail in my roles as Your representative in the lives of my children in Jesus name.
3. Father, let my children make successful progress in their education by doing whatever I tell them regarding Your spiritual and physical plans for their lives.

Tools for Success in Children's Education

"This Book of the Law shall not depart from your mouth, but you shall read [and meditate on] it day and night, so that you may be careful to do [everything] in accordance with all that is written in it; for then you will make your way prosperous, and then you will be successful., (Josh, 1:8, AMP).

"And the Lord was with Hezekiah; he was successful wherever he went. And he rebelled against the king of Assyria and refused to serve him" (2 Kings 2:18, AMP).

There is one word that encapsulates all that is responsible for our family's success in our children's education, and that word is none other than GOD: God the Father, God the Son, God the Holy Spirit. Although our children's educational journeys endured their ups and downs, God has remained faithful, and He has never left us or forsaken us as indicated in the scripture above.

We are all grateful to God for the journey so far. Like Apostle Paul, we can say, *"I am convinced and confident of this very thing, that He who has begun a good work in you will [continue to] perfect and complete it until the day of Christ Jesus [the time of His return] (Phil 1:6, AMP). We are encouraged that God will never leave us or forsake us, according to His promise (Heb. 13:4).* Below, we present seven major strategies that, by God's grace, have proven helpful in our children's educations. Each family is unique, and we recommend that any parents considering these strategies exercise caution, modifying the strategies as appropriate based on their own family's unique situation.

Strategy #1: Putting God First

Any believer who wants to succeed at anything must let God be the driver of their "vehicle of success," to guarantee safe arrival at their expected destination. The inevitability of God's involvement in achieving success is alluded to by the words of Jesus: *"Without me ye can do nothing"*

(John 15:5). Jesus declared, *"I am the Alpha and Omega, the beginning and the ending, the Almighty" (Rev. 1:8)*. Our family has embraced the fact that only God has the power to make anything happen. Our family name, "Olorunnipa," means "God is powerful," or "God is mighty," and we have strived to rely on Him in everything we do, including educating our children. Admittedly, we have not always done this effectively, and we have probably failed a number of times. In general, however, we all have a strong awareness of the need for God in our lives, and we endeavor to call on Him to grant us success in all that we attempt.

While success in general, and education in particular is good, salvation through faith in Jesus Christ is of much greater value. The Bible says, *"what shall it profit a man, if he shall gain the whole world, and lose his own soul?" (Mark 8:36)*. Salvation has eternal, incalculable value, while success is temporary and finite. If one enjoys every worldly success in this life without salvation through Jesus Christ, the Bible says that such a person will be condemned and sent to burn forever in the lake of fire (Mk. 16:16; Rev 21:8). Anyone seeking success in life should begin by seeking salvation through Jesus Christ. The Bible tells us clearly that if we put God first, other things we are looking for will be granted us (Matt. 6:33). By God's grace, everyone in our family has accepted Jesus Christ as our Lord and Savior. We are building our success on Jesus Christ, and you can do the same. If you or your children have not done so, you can receive salvation today, right now, and begin your journey of eternal success. You can begin right now, by praying the following prayer of salvation:

Lord Jesus, thank You for dying for sinners like me. Today, I confess that I am a sinner, and I believe in my heart that You are the Son of God who died and was raised by Your Father. Please have mercy on me and forgive me all my sins, and give me the grace and power to serve You for the rest of my life. Thank You, Jesus, for answering my prayer.

Strategy #2: Parents in Agreement

Another ingredient that can enhance the raising and educating of children is complete agreement between the children's parents. Even if you are a single parent, you can seek out a reliable person to agree with you in prayer. The Bible is emphatic about the power of agreement, for Jesus Christ declares, *"Again I say unto you, That if two of you shall agree on earth as touching any thing that they shall ask, it shall be done for them of my Father which is in heaven"* (Matt. 18:19).

The power of unity and agreement is also evident in the story of Babel, where all people of the earth had one language and decided to build a city and a tower whose top would reach to heaven. God terminated their mission by confounding their language such that they could no longer understand each other *(Gen 11: 1-9)*. Stressing the power in their agreement, God declared," *Behold, the people is one, and they have all one language; and this they begin to do: and now nothing will be restrained from them, which they have imagined to do"* *(Gen 11:6)*.

Parents who desire success for their children must, through prayer and discussions, be in complete agreement on everything, particularly regarding issues relating to children's education, such as child care, choice of schools, finances, food, fun, discipline, privileges, study time, and so on. Whenever there are differences in opinion, parents should continue to engage in dialogue until they achieve consensus. If necessary, a trusted, reliable, neutral person can be sought out to offer opinions. To the extent possible, any differences that confuse the children or create the impression that one parent loves them while the other withholds love must be avoided.

By God's grace, the two of us have been blessed; we have agreed most of the time regarding our children's educational training and upbringing. Some of the agreements have come at great sacrifice. One in particular involved the need for Florence, the children's mother, to delay her own education in order to focus on providing care and nurturing for the children when they were young. During this time, Zacch was extremely busy studying for his doctorate degree, and we did not have the luxury of having family members or nannies to help us care for the children as we did in Nigeria. To the glory of God, our agreement on this matter worked out very well, and Florence was able to make tremendous contributions in terms of laying a solid foundation for our children's education. Not all families are the same, but agreement is always possible, and it will always provide significant benefits in any family.

Strategy #3: Family Team Effort

Every family has a reservoir of resources (intellect, ingenuity, innovation, skills, techniques, organizational ability), which, when properly harnessed and directed, can exceed greatly what any individual family member can achieve by him or herself. The word of God confirms this notion. For example, God in His creation knew that Adam could achieve more if he had help. God therefore declared, *"It is not good that the man should be alone; I will make him an help meet for him."* Consequently, God created Eve to be Adam's wife (Gen 2: 18-23). Still stressing the value of team effort, King Solomon declared that *"Two are better than one; because they have a good reward for their labour" (Eccl. 4:9).*

Our family is very cohesive and supportive of each other. As parents, we have tried to discourage destructive rivalry amongst our children. We are blessed to have instilled cooperation in them so that we did not need to spend wasteful effort on separating fights.

As soon as we discovered the strength of one of our children in a particular area (in math, for example), we have made efforts to help that child sharpen the skill and motivate him or her to become a "sibling mentor" to whomever in the family needs help in that subject area.

Another element that has proven effective in enhancing educational success is celebrating accomplishments together. We encourage any honor or award won by any member of the family to be perceived as a win by the entire family. This creates a strong sense of family cohesiveness.

Strategy #4: Setting Clear Expectations

Expectations refer to that which one looks forward to, what one hopes for. Without expectations, results may be difficult or impossible to achieve. Expectations are pervasive, and they apply to nearly every facet of life. For example, someone who sets out to travel somewhere has an expectation of reaching their destination. For a believer, however, faith, work, and prayer are necessary conditions for expectations to manifest into reality.

The quality of expectations will usually determine the results. For example, high expectations are likely to produce high levels of success, and vice versa. A study conducted by the Harvard Family Research Project indicates that high expectations in school lead to high performance (Parker, 2017). As parents, we had, and still have, high expectations concerning our children's success in education and other areas. In our hearts and by prayer, these expectations are committed unto God claiming His promise that says, *"For surely there is an end; and thine expectation shall not be cut off" (Psalm 23:18).*

As part of planning your children's educations, set clear, unambiguous expectations for each child in each subject, along with other activities they are involved in. Ensure that each child is involved in the process. Evaluate periodically the progress made by each child in each subject relative to the expectations. Give appropriate advice, encouragement, and help as needed to facilitate achieving each expectation. If a child needs help, start within the family to determine whether an older child can help the younger sibling overcome their challenges.

When expectations are backed by specific actions to be taken to achieve them, a plan emerges. Implementing the plan successfully produces the expected outcome. As the saying goes, "fail to plan, plan to fail." Failing to have expectations and plans amounts to planning for failure. At the beginning of every academic season, we would articulate great expectations as to each one of our children's academic success. Then we would start planning how to translate the expectations into reality.

Strategy #5: Moderating Use of TV And Social Media

Television and social media are double-edged sword technologies that can enhance or retard children's educational success because they come with distinct advantages and disadvantages. Some of the advantages often cited include the fact that gadgets, when used with appropriate programs, can increase knowledge, educational enrichment, entertainment, opportunities to view or participate in discussions of social issues, and so on. On the other hand, some of the potential harmful influence of TV and social media include addiction, wasted study time, exposure to violent behavior, passivity and obesity, reduced communication among family members, and exposing users to the risk of harm from pornography.

The two-edged nature of TV and social media as outlined above suggests the need for proper monitoring of children in the use of technology to ensure that they have beneficial rather than detrimental effects on their education. Parents must take leadership in this area to ensure that these technologies do not derail their children's education and social development.

In our family, Television posed the greatest challenge, largely because our limited funds essentially blocked our access to social media. When we noticed that the children were watching television too much, their father tried hiding the remote control. This was not effective as, after he left home, the children would find the remote or simply turn on the TV manually. It got to the point that Zacch started removing the TV cable every day and taking it with him to his office. In the evening, when he returned home, he would reconnect the cable, and the family would watch TV together for a limited time before study time.

Another helpful thing their mother did was to point out positive things to the children whenever they watched TV together. For example, she would explain that the actors on TV shows were hardworking, creative professionals who had little or no time to watch TV. In this way, she was subtly challenging the children to be creative and prepare to work hard to achieve success and be that the kind of people who others would be inspired to watch someday.

Strategy #6: Promotional Tools for Success

Providing incentives to motivate children to succeed in their school work can be very effective. *As the Bible says, God rewards obedience and diligence in serving Him (Deut. 28:1-14; Heb 11:6).* Parents can activate their children's drive to succeed as each child is wired for success. *When God created man and woman in His own image, he declared that they were "very good" (Gen 1:26-31).* Success is part of the goodness that God instilled in man. Oftentimes the drive to success may lie dormant until it is actuated. A case in point can be seen in Apostle Paul's statement to his spiritual protégé, Timothy, *"Wherefore, I put thee in remembrance that thou stir up the gift of God, which is in thee by the putting on of my hands" (1 Tim. 1:6).* As this scripture indicates, Paul was helping Timothy stir up the gift of God in him by providing the "incentive" of laying his hands on Timothy.

Our family has used various types of rewards and incentives (gifts, words of praise, money, restaurant dinners) to motivate our children to work to succeed. Factors such as the child's age, interest, level of education, and availability of resources (material, financial, etc.) dictated what the rewards would be. Of course, money turned out to be the most popular incentive. No wonder the Bible declares, *"money answereth all things" (Eccl.10:19).*

Sometimes, at the beginning of the school term, Zacch would commit to each of our children that he would pay $5 for every "A" on their report cards. This worked like magic. At the end of the term, the children brought home report cards almost full of A's.

Other incentives we used to motivate our children for academic success include:
- Taking them to theme parks
- Ice cream and other treats
- Buying them educational electronic gadgets (when affordable)
- Family cook out

Strategy #7: Preparing for College Life and Beyond

Education is a lifelong endeavor, although formal education is segmented into levels. Most of what has been discussed thus far has focused mainly on children training in elementary-to-high-school levels. The older children are, and the further along they are in their education, the more independent they become, including parents' inputs to their educational choices and progress. However, parents must remain interested and involved in their children's education.

Find out from your children as early as possible what their interests are, what careers they might want to consider, and why. Then, help them identify what types of classes will be required to support their choices so that adequate preparation can be made to ensure that they have the necessary preparation for their preferred careers. Parents must also ensure that their children receive appropriate counseling at school. If necessary, visit your child's teachers and guidance counselor to ensure that all ground is covered in terms of meeting college requirements.

By the time our children reached their final year of high school, they had become much more familiar with the American educational system than either of their parents. They were very proactive in seeking out the necessary information in preparing for college. They ensured that they were prepared for standardized tests such as the PSAT and SAT. They researched colleges and how to put together strong application packages.

By the grace of God, all four of our children were admitted to Ivy League Schools, several with multiple admissions. As parents, we focused on providing the necessary support and praying for them. Obviously, these achievements were made possible only through God's grace. As the scripture says, it is *"Not by might, nor by power, but by my spirit, saith the Lord of hosts" (Zech. 4:6)*. God did it, and we are immensely grateful to Him. We are proud of our children because they have made our work as parents relatively easy and worth all the sacrifices we made.

End of Chapter Prayer Points
1. Father, please remove from my children anything (TV, social media) that will stand as stumbling blocks to their success in education and in other areas of life.
2. Holy Spirit, teach me how best to encourage my children to excel in education.
3. Father, let my children respond positively to any incentive I provide for them to do well in their studies.
4. 4 Father, please increase my capacity to stir up and water the seed of success in my children.

Praying for and Prophesying Over Your Children

"Thou shalt also decree a thing, and it shall be established unto thee: and the light shall shine upon thy ways" (Pro. 22:28).

The ability to speak, pray, and prophesy are privileges that God has given believers to enable them to communicate with Him and make their needs and wishes known. God has promised to provide answers to all requests made to Him by prayers of faith (Matt 7:7, Mark 11:24, Isa 65:24). Praying and prophesying based on the word and spirit of God can produce great results, given God's promise, *"Call unto me, and I will answer thee, and show thee great and mighty things, which thou knowest not" (Jer. 33:3)*. Success in education is part of the favor God can bestow upon His followers.

There is tremendous power in God's spoken word, as the author of the book of Hebrews pointed out: *"For the word of God is quick, and powerful, and sharper than any two edged sword, piercing even to the dividing asunder of soul and spirit, and of the joints and marrow, and is a discerner of the thoughts and intents of the heart"* (Heb. 4:12). Plausible evidence of the power of God's word is His creation of heaven and earth through spoken words (Gen. 1: 1-31). The power in God's word can be harnessed through prayer and prophetic utterances to call forth the things we want to manifest in our lives and those of our children, including educational success.

"Prophesying," as used in this chapter, refers to speaking blessings and making inspired declarations over children regarding their destinies. Christian parents have possibly the best opportunity to pray for and prophesy over their children. There are several examples in the Bible of parental prophetic declarations to their children, some positive (blessings), and some negative (curses). The pace setter in this regard is God, the supreme parent of all human beings. When God created Adam and Eve, He declared to them, *"Be fruitful, and multiply, and replenish the earth, and subdue it" (Gen 1:28)*. God declared repeatedly to Abraham that his seed, or offspring, will be instruments of blessing for the entire world (Gen. 12:3; 18:18; 22:16-18). Isaac, Abraham's son, also pronounced blessings on his own sons, Jacob and Essau (Gen 27). Jacob had 12 sons, and toward the end of his life, he prophesied on each of them (Gen 49).

Noah is the first human being recorded in the Bible who made prophetic declarations over his children, as reflected in the following scripture:

"And Noah began to be an husbandman, and he planted a vineyard: And he drank of the wine, and was drunken; and he was uncovered within his tent. And Ham, the father of Canaan, saw the nakedness of his father, and told his two brethren without. And Shem and Japheth took a garment, and laid it upon both their shoulders, and went backward, and covered the nakedness of their father; and their faces were backward, and they saw not their father's nakedness. And Noah awoke from his wine, and knew what his younger son had done unto him. And he said, Cursed be Canaan; a servant of servants shall he be unto his brethren. And he said, Blessed be the Lord God of Shem; and Canaan shall be his servant. God shall enlarge Japheth, and he shall dwell in the tents of Shem; and Canaan shall be his servant". (Gen 9:20-27)

From this story, we can see that Noah cursed Canaan, descendant of Ham, because Noah believed that Ham dishonored him by seeing his nakedness. On the other hand, Noah blessed Shem and Japheth, who honored him by covering him without seeing his nakedness. Some Bible scholars have suggested that the declarations of Noah against Ham (Genesis 9:20–25) was fulfilled centuries later when the Israelites entered the land of Canaan and subdued the inhabitants of that land (1 Kings 9:20–21). Similarly, Noah's declaration on Shem and Japheth were also fulfilled as Shem became the ancestor of the Semitic peoples with Abraham (a descendant of Shem) being the first person in the Bible referred to as a "Hebrew" (Genesis 10:1, 21–31 and 14:13).

Parents who want their children to succeed in education and other areas can borrow a leaf from God, Abraham, Isaac, and Jacob, and prophesy regularly over those children. Regrettably, some parents, rain curses instead of blessings over their children, even for minor offences. Such parents forget that words have power. If demonic agents hear curses, they can manipulatively stamp such curses on the children and tarnish their destinies. If you have been a victim of such curses, you need deliverance to break the curses. Cry to Jesus, who alone can revoke them. We urge parents to prophesy blessings over your children frequently. Remember, the Bible says, *"Death and life are in the power of the tongue: and they that love it shall eat the fruit thereof" (Pro 18:21)*. Prophesy life and success to the education of your children so that they can produce fruits of success for your family to harvest.

HOW TO PRAY FOR AND PROPHESY OVER CHILDREN

While there are no hard and fast rules on how to pray and prophesy over children for educational success., the following guidelines are suggested for considerations:

- Precede prayer with praise
- Pray to God for guidance on how to proceed
- Be Bible-based in your approach
- Seek counsel from your Pastor and/or trusted ordained minister
- Start early (before or during conception, at birth, or soon after birth)
- Be in agreement with your spouse in prayer
- Let the child be aware that you are praying for him/her
- Lay hands on the child while praying and prophesying
- Track the manifestation of your prophesies and testify
- Sow seeds/make vows specifically with respect to destiny fulfillment of the child
- Give thanks to God for answering your prayers
- Prophesy regularly over your children

Praying for and Prophesying Over Your Children

Our children were prayed and prophesied over directly or indirectly from the time of conception. From time to time, we still do this, even now that they are grown up. We encourage parents who are not yet prophesying over their children to begin doing so immediately. You shall testify to the goodness of God. Note that you can also teach your children who are of age to prophesy over you as a parent for the Bible says, *"Iron sharpeneth iron; so a man sharpeneth the countenance of his friend" (Pro 27:17).*

Prophetic Prayer Points for Children

1. Farther, thank You for the family You have given me.
2. Lord Jesus, thank You for my salvation and that of my family members.
3. Father, thank You for the good plans You have for me and my family (Jer. 29:11).
4. My child, (name him/her) you shall be trained in the way of the Lord and you will not depart from that path in Jesus name (Pro. 22:6).
5. Father, I and the children whom You have given me are for signs and for wonders, in Jesus' mighty name (Isa, 8:18).
6. Father, I declare that all my children will serve you diligently, in Jesus' name. (Ex. 23:25).
7. Father, all my children shall be taught of the Lord and great shall be their peace in Jesus name (Isa. 54:13).
8. Father, according to Your word, no weapon fashioned against my children shall prosper in Jesus' mighty name (Isa. 54:71).
9. Father, by Your grace, it shall be well and perfect with my children, in Jesus name (Isa. 3:10; Psalm 138:8).
10. Father, my children shall increase in wisdom and in stature after the order of Jesus Christ (Luke 2:52).

11. Father, my children shall find favor and mercy wherever they go and in whatever they do, in Jesus name (Gen 39:6, 21; Luke 2:52; Est 2:17, 5:2).
12. Father, based on Your word, I decree that my children shall have more understanding than all their teachers and they shall still be humble (Psalm. 119:99).
13. Holy Spirit You will be the ultimate Teacher for my children who will bring all things to their remembrance in Jesus name (Jn 14:26).
14. My child, (name him/her) as you go to school, God will give you knowledge and skill in all learning and wisdom like Daniel in Jesus name (Dan. 1:17)
15. I decree and declare that, (name him/her) shall be head and not tail Deut. 28:13).
16. Father, all my children shall be obedient and greatly rewarded in Jesus name (Deut. 28:1-14).
17. My child, (name him/her) you shall be filled with the spirit of God, in wisdom, and in understanding, and in knowledge, and in all studies and activities (Ex. 31:3).
18. My children shall have sound mind and shall not be tormented by the spirit of fear in Jesus name (1 Tim 1:17).
19. My children are blessed and shall be mighty upon the earth (Psalm 112:2).
20. The destiny of my children shall not be truncated, in Jesus name (Isa.54:17).
21. All evil decrees and curses against my children shall return to the senders (Isa. 10:1).
22. My child, (name) anointing to be the best among your equals shall be upon you in Jesus name (Deut. 12:13).
23. My children shall not be wicked nor worthless like Eli's sons, they will know God and be a blessing to their generation in Jesus name (1 Sam 2:12, Acts 13:36).

Praying for and Prophesying Over Your Children

24. My child, (name him/her) you will study well and you will never fail any exam in the mighty name of God (1 Tim 2:15, Josh. 1:5).
25. Jehovah Jireh will supply all my need and money will not be an obstacle to my children education in the mighty name of Jesus (Phil 4:19).
26. The God that opens door that no one can shut will grant my children admission to the best schools they desire anywhere in the world in Jesus name (Rev. 3:7, 8).
27. My God will order the steps of my children and delight in their ways in all educational pursuits and career choices in Jesus name (Psalm 37:23).
28. You spirit of anxiety and confusion; my children are out of your reach in the mighty name of Jesus (Phil. 4:6).
29. I decree divine protection over my children as they go to and from school; and in all other places in Jesus mighty name (Psalm 91).
30. My children shall not be prone to spirit of error in their school work and in all other activities (Psalm 19:2, 1 John 4:6).
31. Power that causes brain block during examinations shall not have any influence over my children in Jesus name (1 Chron 4:10; Psalm 119:15).
32. My expectation concerning the educational success of my children shall not be cut short in Jesus name (Pro 23:18;' 24:14).
33. My children's educational performance shall glorify God and advertise His goodness in Jesus name (1 Chron 16:29).
34. Any documents carrying the names of my children with any positive request shall receive easy approval in Jesus name (John 14:14).
35. I prophesy that any power that frustrates and/or destroys destinies shall fail concerning my children's education (Pro 26:2, ERV).

36. My children shall not be lazy concerning their education, they shall be diligent and prosperous in the mighty name of Jesus (Pro 10:4; 22:29).
37. People of influence and prominence will speak in favor of my children regarding their education and other pursuits (Acts 5: 34-42).
38. Whatever I prophesy over children shall come to pass quickly in the name of Jesus.
39. My labor and that of my children in all our endeavors shall be profitable in Jesus name (Psalm 127:1).
40. The wickedness of the wicked shall not prevail over my children (Ps. 7:9).
41. My children shall not belong to any unprofitable association in Jesus name, (2 Cor. 6: 14).
42. My children will not make choices that will lead them to troubles, in Jesus name (Deut. 30:19).
43. Academically and otherwise, any help my children need for success shall be readily available, in Jesus name (Isa, 41:10, Heb. 4:16).
44. I decree that my children shall not listen to the counsel of the ungodly (Psalm 1:1).
45. I declare that my children shall be mentally focused and excel in their education.
46. The harvest that will accrue to my children in education and in other areas shall be bountiful in Jesus name (2 Cor. 9:6).
47. My children shall not labor for others to reap at their expense in Jesus name (Isa. 65: 25).
48. The Lord will lead my children in choice of extracurricular activities that will enhance their educational success in Jesus name (Psalm 32:8).
49. I decree that my children shall not die young, but shall live their full age (Ex. 23:26b).

50. Father, thank You for I know You will manifest these prophesies and many more in the lives of my children in Jesus name (Eph 3:20).

RAISING SUCCESSFUL CHILDREN:

A Guide for Christian Parents

God is very interested in both the spiritual and physical welfare of children because they are His heritage (Psalm 127:3). No wonder the inspired word of God says, *"Train up a child in the way he should go: and when he is old, he will not depart from it". (Pro 22:6).* With respect to the *modus operandi* of training children, the LORD is the ultimate model, being a Teacher of children Himself (Isaiah 54:13). Naturally, parents are God's number one choice when it comes to raising and training children. It is a great privilege, and at the same time quite challenging to be responsible for "Godly seed", or "God's Heritage" or people Jesus Christ described as "- - of such is the king-dom of heaven" (Matt 19:14).

Raising Successful Children is written as a valuable resource to aid parents in nurturing the "seed of success" in their children to achieve desirable results that will meet God's plans for children and, at the same time, prepare those children for productive careers beneficial to their families and to the society at large. Based on God's words and the authors' wealth of experiences in raising and training children, proven strategies, tips and suggestions are presented in this book to help parents achieve phenomenal results in training their children for educational success. With God's help, Zacch and Florence have successfully raised their four children and each one of is an Ivy-league graduate. Glory be to God!

About the Authors

Zacch and Florence Olorunnipa are Pastors of the Redeemed Christian Church of God, Go Ye Chapel, Tallahassee, Florida. For more than 20 years, God has been using them to transform and upgrade lives through many ways, including, writing books, speaking engagements, counselling, giving hope to the hopeless, helping the helpless, ministering to and providing support to widows and orphans indifferent parts of the world.

Zacch I. Olorunnipa is a retired Professor of Agricultural Economics and Agribusiness. Florence O. Olorunnipa is a Registered Nurse. They are blessed with four wonderful children (Funmi, Shola, Toluse and Yemi).

www.ingramcontent.com/pod-product-compliance
Lightning Source LLC
Chambersburg PA
CBHW052044070526
44584CB00018B/2600